This book is a

Gift

From

....

To

....

Date

....

May God bless you through this book

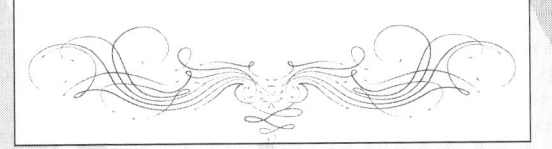

Prayers to heal broken relationship

PRAYERS TO HEAL BROKEN RELATIONSHIP

PRAYERS TO HEAL BROKEN RELATIONSHIP

Copyright © 2014

PRAYER M. MADUEKE

ISBN:9781500163709

Prayer Publications

All rights reserved. No part of this work may be reproduced or transmitted in any form or by any means without written permission from the publisher

Unless otherwise indicated, all Scripture quotations are taken from the King James Version of the Bible, and used by permission. All emphasis within quotations is the author's additions.

First Edition, 2014

For further information of permission

1 Babatunde close, off Olaitan Street, Surulere, Lagos, Nigeria
+234 803 353 0599
Email: pastor@prayermadueke.com,
Website: www.prayermadueke.com

Dedication

This book is dedicated to people who are trusting God to heal their broken or strained relationship. The Lord who sees your sincere dedication will answer your prayers
Amen.

Prayers to heal broken relationship

BOOK OVERVIEW

PRAYERS TO HEAL BROKEN RELATIONSHIP

- *The crying of blood*
- *Blood cries against unborn generation*
- *The bloody family*
- *What makes a family bloody?*
- *What is idolatry?*
- *What is a covenant?*
- *Why did God design covenant?*
- *What happens when blood cries out?*

THE CRYING OF BLOOD

In a general sense, relationship is the way in which two or more people or organizations regard and behave toward each other. Whether it is human or organizational relationship, same principles abound. There are things that destroy relationships fast. One of such is the cry of blood in the foundation of a person or an organization.

When there is blood crying out against any person or organization, it is difficult to achieve anything useful in relationship. Crying of blood can empower witches and wizards to fight against people with ease.

> *And Cain talked with Abel his brother: and it came to pass, when they were in the field, that Cain rose up against Abel his brother, and slew him. And the LORD said unto Cain, Where is Abel thy brother? And he said, I know not: Am I my brother's keeper? And he said, What hast thou done? The voice of thy brother's blood crieth unto me from the ground. And now art thou cursed from the earth, which hath opened her mouth to receive thy brother's blood from thy hand; When thou tillest the ground, it shall not henceforth yield unto thee her strength; a fugitive and a vagabond shalt thou be in the earth. And Cain said unto the LORD, My punishment is greater than I can bear. Behold, thou hast driven me out this day from the face of the earth; and from thy face shall I be hid; and I shall be a fugitive and a vagabond in the earth; and it shall come to pass, that every one that findeth me shall slay me"* (Genesis 4:8-14).

When Cain shed the blood of his younger brother, Abel, God cursed his life on earth and he became a fugitive and vagabond. Therefore, his presence scared people away. People got irritated at the sight of Cain. God's presence departed from him. In such case, Cain could do nothing that would make people relate with him any longer because his brother's blood cried against him. The kind of demon that follows a person who shed blood is a chief demon and even legion of demons. People close to murderers do not always know what they pass through because when they shed blood, demons celebrated. That was the case with Cain and Lamech and they complained bitterly.

> *"Behold, thou hast driven me out this day from the face of the earth; and from thy face shall I be hid; and I shall be a fugitive and a vagabond in the earth; and it shall come to pass, that every one that findeth me shall slay me. And Lamech said unto his wives, Adah and Zillah, Hear my voice; ye wives of Lamech, hearken unto my speech: for I have slain a man to my wounding, and a young man to my hurt. If Cain shall be avenged sevenfold, truly Lamech seventy and sevenfold"* (Genesis 4:14, 23-24).

God hates bloodshed and when blood is shed, His presence departs. At other times, demons that influenced murder overwhelm murderers so fast. Whenever blood is shed, it goes to God to lodge complaint against the person that shed it.

> *"And he said, What hast thou done? The voice of thy brother's blood crieth unto me from the ground. And now art thou cursed from the earth, which hath opened her mouth to receive thy brother's blood from thy hand"* (Genesis 4:10-11).

BLOOD CRIES AGAINST UNBORN GENERATION

The cry of innocent blood has no limit of space or time. It can cry against a generation forever and ever.

> "And it came to pass, when Ahab heard that Naboth was dead, that Ahab rose up to go down to the vineyard of Naboth the Jezreelite, to take possession of it. And the word of the LORD came to Elijah the Tishbite, saying, Arise, go down to meet Ahab king of Israel, which is in Samaria: behold, he is in the vineyard of Naboth, whither he is gone down to possess it. And thou shalt speak unto him, saying, Thus saith the LORD, Hast thou killed, and also taken possession? And thou shalt speak unto him, saying, Thus saith the LORD, In the place where dogs licked the blood of Naboth shall dogs lick thy blood, even thine. And Ahab said to Elijah, Hast thou found me, O mine enemy? And he answered, I have found thee: because thou hast sold thyself to work evil in the sight of the LORD. Behold, I will bring evil upon thee, and will take away thy posterity, and will cut off from Ahab him that pisseth against the wall, and him that is shut up and left in Israel, And will make thine house like the house of Jeroboam the son of Nebat, and like the house of Baasha the son of Ahijah, for the provocation wherewith thou hast provoked me to anger, and made Israel to sin. And of Jezebel also spake the LORD, saying, The dogs shall eat Jezebel by the wall of Jezreel. Him that dieth of Ahab in the city the dogs shall eat; and him that dieth in the field shall the fowls of the air eat" (1 Kings 21:16-24).

When the family of Ahab shed the blood of Naboth, it was as if nothing happened. Jezebel informed her husband, Ahab, to go and take possession of Naboth's vineyard. However, as he entered the land, he met prophet Elijah, who confronted him saying, 'Hast thou killed, and also taken possession? In the place where dogs licked the blood of Naboth, shall dogs lick thy blood.'

It was an open confrontation and release of multiple curses on Ahab and his household. These curses put Ahab's entire household into generational bondage. The blood of Naboth cried against the family of Ahab until God avenged. We know that Ahab later regretted the murder of Naboth and humbled himself before God.

> "But there was none like unto Ahab, which did sell himself to work wickedness in the sight of the LORD, whom Jezebel his wife stirred up. And he did very abominably in following idols, according to all things as did the Amorites, whom the LORD cast out before the children of Israel. And it came to pass, when Ahab heard those words, that he rent his clothes, and put sackcloth upon his flesh, and fasted, and lay in sackcloth, and went softly. And the word of the LORD came to Elijah the Tishbite, saying, Seest thou how Ahab humbleth himself before me? Because he humbleth himself before me, I will not bring the evil in his days: but in his son's days will I bring the evil upon his house." (1 Kings 21:25-29).

Because of Ahab's prayers, the family enjoyed peace for a few more years. The point is that God heard Ahab's prayer. Therefore, if you are coming from a family that shed innocent blood, you can repent as Ahab did and separate yourself from your family's bondage. Otherwise, you suffer the consequence of your family's evil deed.

> *"And they continued three years without war between Syria and Israel"* (1 Kings 22:1).

> *"And when Jehu was come to Jezreel, Jezebel heard of it; and she painted her face, and tired her head, and looked out at a window. And as Jehu entered in at the gate, she said,* Had Zimri peace, who slew his master? *And he lifted up his face to the window, and said, Who is on my side? Who? And there looked out to him two or three eunuchs. And he said, Throw her down. So they threw her down: and some of her blood was sprinkled on the wall, and on the horses: and he trode her under foot. And when he was come in, he did eat and drink, and said, Go, see now this cursed woman, and bury her: for she is a king's daughter. And they went to bury her: but they found no more of her than the skull, and the feet, and the palms of her hands. Wherefore they came again, and told him. And he said, This is the word of the LORD, which he spake by his servant Elijah the Tishbite, saying, In the portion of Jezreel shall dogs eat the flesh of Jezebel: And the carcass of Jezebel shall be as dung upon the face of the field in the portion of Jezreel; so that they shall not say, This is Jezebel"* (2 Kings 9:30-37).

> *"And it came to pass, when the letter came to them, that they took the king's sons, and slew seventy persons, and put their heads in baskets, and sent him them to Jezreel"* (2 Kings 10:7).

It is very difficult to be successful in relating with other people when blood is crying against you or your family. You will not prevail in any business or work. If you do not handle the issue of blood crying against you, you will continue to suffer. Even true believers whose families shed innocent blood need to do something to be free.

> *"Then there was a famine in the days of David three years, year after year; and David enquired of the LORD. And the LORD answered, It is for Saul, and for his bloody house, because he slew the Gibeonites. And the king called the Gibeonites, and said unto them; (now the Gibeonites were not of the children of Israel, but of the remnant of the Amorites; and the children of Israel had sworn unto them: and Saul sought to slay them in his zeal to the children of Israel and Judah.) Wherefore David said unto the Gibeonites, What shall I do for you? And wherewith shall I make the atonement, that ye may bless the inheritance of the LORD?"* (2 Samuel 21:1-3).

In the days of David, the entire nation of Israel, including David, suffered for three years because blood cried against them. Though David was not guilty of the crime, however, as soon as he ascended the throne, Israel experienced severe famine for three years. He could not trace the cause of their suffering until after three years.

For three solid years, the whole nation of Israel experienced dire suffering and hardship. It was at the third year that David went into serious prayers of enquiry. Then the Lord revealed the cause of the famine. Had David prayed earlier, the famine would have not lasted for three years. If he did not pray at all, the famine would have continued for more years.

The lesson here is that blood can also cry against good Christians. There may be things you need to do to free yourself to enjoy successful relationship. Without allowing God to reveal such things to you, you may remain miserable and unable to marry even when you have the assurance of heaven and salvation.

This same thing happened to David and the nation of Israel. If the blood of an uncircumcised Gideonite could hold a whole nation to ransom, then your family, city, etc., could not be better or more precious than the nation of Israel. If God could not spare David and the children of Israel, then God will surely hold you or your family accountable for any shed blood. However, the good news was that immediately David prayed, God answered and revealed the cause of the famine to him.

One may wonder why David did not pray until after three years. Actually, David prayed but he did not pray the right prayers. In your own case, could it be that you have been praying wrong prayers? However, when David prayed the right prayers, God heard him. Likewise, when you pray the right prayers God will hear you.

THE BLOODY FAMILY

Saul and his family killed the Gibeonites and the whole nation of Israel would later suffer the consequence for three years, including David and his family. Who were the Gibeonites? The Gibeonites deceitfully made a covenant of peace with Israel. However, when the children of Israel discovered their deceit, it was too late.

> *"And Joshua made peace with them, and made a league with them, to let them live: and the princes of the congregation swore unto them. And Joshua called for them, and he spake unto them, saying, Wherefore have ye beguiled us, saying, We are very far from you; when ye dwell among us? Now therefore ye are cursed, and there shall none of you be freed from being bondmen, and hewers of wood and drawers of water for the house of my God. And Joshua made them that day hewers of wood and drawers of water for the congregation, and for the altar of the LORD, even unto this day, in the place which he should choose"* (Joshua 9:15, 22, 23, 27).

The Gibeonites tricked Joshua to enter into covenant of peace with them. He made the princes of the congregation to swear to the Gibeonites. Later, when Joshua found out the truth, he cursed the Gibeonites because of their unfaithfulness.

Many years later, Saul broke that covenant by destroying the Gibeonites and it affected the whole nation of Israel. It could be possible that you are not the cause of your present suffering and repeated failures in relationships. Nevertheless, it is your responsibility to pray and inquire of the Lord for the sake of your deliverance.

> *"Our fathers have sinned, and are not; and we have borne their iniquities. Servants have ruled over us: there is none that doth deliver us out of their hand. We gat our bread with the peril of our lives because of the sword of the wilderness. Our skin was black like an oven because of the terrible famine. They ravished the women in Zion, and the maids in the cities of Judah. Princes are hanged up by their hand: the faces of elders were not honored. They took the young men to grind, and the children fell under the wood. The elders have ceased from the gate, the young men from their music. The joy of our heart is ceased; our dance is turned into mourning. The crown is fallen from our head: woe unto us that we have sinned! For this our heart is faint; for these things our eyes are dim"* (Lamentation 5:7-17).

Proverbs 26:2 reveals that *"The curse causeless shall not come."* Therefore, there must be a reason for whatever that is going on in your life. If your family were bloody, then you would suffer failures in relationships.

WHAT MAKES A FAMILY BLOODY?

- When a member of the family sheds blood, the family becomes bloody

- When a member of the family commits abortion, the family becomes bloody

- When a member of the family performs blood or animal sacrifice, the family becomes bloody

- When a member of the family offers blood sacrifice to any idol, the family becomes bloody

    "And God spake all these words, saying, ²I am the LORD thy God, which have brought thee out of the land of Egypt, out of the house of bondage. Thou shalt have no other gods before me. Thou shalt not make unto thee any graven image, or any likeness of any thing that is in heaven above, or that is in the earth beneath, or that is in the water under the earth: Thou shalt not bow down thyself to them, nor serve them: for I the LORD thy God am a jealous God, visiting the iniquity of the fathers upon the children unto the third and fourth generation of them that hate me" (Exodus 20:1-5).

Idolatry separates man from God. It destroys relationships quickly. Family's ancestors can severe relationship between their unborn children and God through idolatry.

WHAT IS IDOLATRY?

- Idolatry is bowing down to images
- It is sacrificing to other gods
- It is fearing other gods
- It is worshipping other gods
- It is trying to worship God through an image
- It is sacrificing to images
- It is swearing by other gods
- It is walking after other gods
- It is looking up to other gods
- It is serving other gods with your resources
- It is worshipping angels
- It is worshipping the hosts of heaven
- It is worshipping devil
- It is setting up of idols in your heart
- It is worshipping of dead people
- It is covetousness and sensuality
- It is worshipping symbols instead of God

> "Therefore the people came to Moses, and said, We have sinned, for we have spoken against the LORD, and against thee; pray unto the LORD,

that he take away the serpents from us. And Moses prayed for the people. And the LORD said unto Moses, Make thee a fiery serpent, and set it upon a pole: and it shall come to pass, that every one that is bitten, when he looketh upon it, shall live. And Moses made a serpent of brass, and put it upon a pole, and it came to pass, that if a serpent had bitten any man, when he beheld the serpent of brass, he lived" (Numbers 21:7-9).

While most Africans and Asians worship idols in the above-mentioned ways, westerners worship idols through the following ways:

1. Possession - Matthew 6:19-21, 24-33

2. Plenty - Luke 12:15-21, Colossians 3:5

3. Pride - Acts 12:30-23, 2 Timothy 3:1-2

4. People - Matthew 10:37, John 9:18-23, 5:44

5. Pleasure - 2 Timothy 3:1-2, 1 John 2:15-17

If you are serious about restoring lost relationships, then deal with issues of idolatry and blood crying in your bloodline. These two things bring curses upon people. These curses ruin people's chances to enjoy successful relationships. They also keep people out of God's presence and from the reach of their divine helpers. If you fail to overcome these two things, you could remain a victim, even as a true Christian.

WHAT IS A COVENANT?

- A covenant is a mutual understanding between two or more parties, each binding itself to fulfill specific obligations.

- It is also a legal contract.

- It is a binding agreement to do or not to do specified things.

WHY DID GOD DESIGN COVENANT?

- God designed covenant to establish friendship (*See* 1 Samuel 18:3).

- To establish basis for mutual protection and benefit (*See* Genesis 26:28-29).

- To guarantee alliance or assistance in time of war (*See* 1 Kings 15:18).

A fact about covenant is that as soon as it is confirmed, it becomes unutterable or irrevocable.

> *"And I will put enmity between thee and the woman, and between thy seed and her seed; it shall bruise thy head, and thou shalt bruise his heel"* (Genesis 3:15).

In a covenant, legal representative represents self, the people and the children (born and unborn) from generation to generation. Unless you break such covenants publicly or with the other party, you remain bound and suffer consequences, even when you are a true Christian.

Christian life qualifies you to resist devil through the help of Jesus Christ. That is why James admonished that we must resist the devil for him to flee. Likewise, Paul likened Christian life to fighting a warfare and wrestling.

> *"For we wrestle not against flesh and blood, but against principalities, against powers, against the rulers of the darkness of this world, against spiritual wickedness in high places"* (Ephesians 6:12).

> *"Fight the good fight of faith, lay hold on eternal life, where unto thou art also called, and hast professed a good profession before many witnesses"* (1 Timothy 6:12).

> *"For though we walk in the flesh, we do not war after the flesh:(For the weapons of our warfare are not carnal, but mighty through God to the pulling down of strong holds;) Casting down imaginations, and every high thing that exalteth itself against the knowledge of God, and bringing into captivity every thought to the obedience of Christ"* (2 Corinthians 10:3-5).

If you refuse to fight or wrestle, some old things would not leave on their own. Covenant is an irrevocable commitment that you must confront and break. That was what David did when the blood of Abner was approached his throne to cause a personal and national disaster.

> *"And afterward when David heard it, he said, I and my kingdom are guiltless before the LORD for ever from the blood of Abner the son of Ner: Let it rest on the head of Joab, and on all his father's house; and let there not fail from the house of Joab one that hath an issue, or that is a*

leper, or that leaneth on a staff, or that falleth on the sword, or that lacketh bread" (2 Samuel 3:28-29).

The most effective type of covenant is blood covenant. For instance, a person that broke a lady's virginity entered into blood covenant with the lady, which she must break at all cost. Also abortion is a blood covenant whether legalized or not by the state. The blood shed through abortions could cry against nations and destroy nation's relationship with other nations. It can cry against an individual, family or entire nation. Evil covenants or curses can cause various misfortunes. Idolatry and bloodshed are very disastrous.

WHAT HAPPENS WHEN BLOOD CRIES OUT?

- When blood cries, relationships cannot last or yield lasting fruits.

- Hatred and rejection appear in the middle of relationships to abort such relationships.

- Victims are rejected easily, hated and abandoned without convincing reasons.

- Relationships are manipulated or bewitched by satanic agents.

- The character of victims changes for worse and they behave abnormally, even to their own surprise and hurt.

- Hard work cannot yield good result.

- Good relationships cannot last.

- People engage and disengage quickly.

- Marriages suffer divorces and separation.

- Enemies manipulate and control people's relationships.

- Peace disappears and strife abounds.

- Divine helpers disappear and evil helpers dictate extreme conditions to render help.

- People suffer premature deaths.

- People achieve nothing in their lifetimes.

- More people marry late, and others marry wrong person.
- More people end their lives depressed and consider suicide.

THE BEST WAY OUT

- Repent truly and fervently.
- Determine to fight your battle and ask the Holy Spirit to assist you.
- Break all evil covenants and curses from their roots.
- Silence the crying of blood in your foundation.
- Appropriate and invoke the blood of Jesus.
- Withdraw yourself from any bondage.
- Have faith in God.
- Live a holy life
- Endeavour to be baptized with the Holy Spirit with the evidence of speaking in tongues.

PRAYERS TO HEAL BROKEN RELATIONSHIP

Bible References: <u>Matthew 1:18-25</u>, <u>John 15:1-2</u>

Begin with praise and worship

---

1. Father Lord, deliver me from the woes of evil relationships, in the name of Jesus.

2. Any evil personality that is standing between my creator and I, be frustrated, in the name of Jesus.

3. Any power that wants to take the place of Christ in my life, I disengage you, in the name of Jesus.

4. I destroy any evil design to keep me out of good relationships, in the name of Jesus.

5. Let envy and rivalries that exist in my relationships be exposed and disgraced, in the name of Jesus.

6. I break and lose myself from evil dedication that is frustrating my relationships, in the name of Jesus.

7. O Lord, arise and empower me to keep good relationships, in the name of Jesus.

8. Any evil covenant that is frustrating my relationships, break, in the name of Jesus.

9. Father Lord, deliver me from parental curses that are affecting my relationships, in the name of Jesus.

10. I destroy family idols that are waging war against my relationships, in the name of Jesus.

11. I cast out demons that are militating against my relationship, in the name of Jesus.

12. I terminate any fellowship with evil spirits, in the name of Jesus.

13. I deliver myself from inherited bondage of evil relationship, in the name of Jesus.

14. Blood of Jesus, flow into my foundation and deliver me from troubles, in the name of Jesus.

15. Blood of Jesus, flush out evil characters in my life, in the name of Jesus.

16. I destroy evil traits that are scaring good people away from me, in the name of Jesus.

17. Let problems that transferred into my life to destroyed my chances to enjoy good relationships catch fire, in the name of Jesus.

18. Blood of Jesus, cleanse my life from failures of my parents, in the name of Jesus.

19. I cast out spirit of death that is ruining my chances of good relationship with people, in the name of Jesus.

20. I discard any false information that is designed to destroy my relationship, in the name of Jesus.

21. Every satanic monitoring gadget that is fashioned to destroy my relationship, catch fire, in the name of Jesus.

Prayers to heal broken relationship

22. Any evil utterance that was spoken over my relationships, expire, in the name of Jesus.

23. Let resurrection power of Jesus quicken my relationships, in the name of Jesus.

24. I recover every good thing that I have lost in my relationship, in the name of Jesus.

25. I expose strangers that are attacking my successes in relationship, in the name of Jesus.

26. I uproot evil imaginations that are targeting my relationships, in the name of Jesus.

27. Let every destructive plans of my enemies to keep me out of relationships expire, in the name of Jesus.

28. I erase and disband evil information from the heart of my helpers, in the name of Jesus.

29. I cast out the spirit of fear, doubt, and discouragement in my heart, in the name of Jesus.

30. I cancel all ungodly and false information that was gathered against me, in the name of Jesus.

31. Let angels of God restore good relationships that I have lost, in the name of Jesus.

32. I refuse to break my relationship with my divine helpers, in the name of Jesus.

33. O Lord, heal broken relationships that you have designed to help me, in the name of Jesus.

34. Any evil record that was designed to terminate my relationships, catch fire, in the name of Jesus.

35. Any strongman that is standing against my success in relationships, die, in the name of Jesus.

36. I bind and cast out demons that are promoting disagreements in my life, in the name of Jesus.

37. I close every doorway of the enemy into my relationships, in the name of Jesus.

38. I vomit spiritual parasites that are eating deep into my relationship, vomit it now, in the name of Jesus.

39. I break demonic padlocks that were used to lock up my relationship, in the name of Jesus.

40. Let demonic eyes that are monitoring my relationship go blind, in the name of Jesus.

41. Any evil leg that has walked into my relationship, walk out now, in the name of Jesus.

42. O Lord, reactivate my lost relationship opportunities, in the name of Jesus.

43. Let any evil plantation that is growing in my relationship die by fire, in the name of Jesus.

44. Lord Jesus, grant my success in relationships, in the name of Jesus.

45. Any devourer that is eating up my success in relationships, die, in the name of Jesus.

46. Any blood sacrifice that is crying against my relationships, expire, in the name of Jesus.

47. I silence evil voices that are speaking against my relationships, in the name of Jesus.

48. Let any strange personality that has vowed to stand on my way die, in the name of Jesus.

49. I destroy strange behaviors and curses in my relationships, in the name of Jesus.

50. O Lord, arise and heal every wound my relationship has suffered, in the name of Jesus.

Thank You So Much!

Beloved, I hope you enjoyed this book as much as I believe God has touched your heart today. I cannot thank you enough for your continued support for this prayer ministry.

I appreciate you so much for taking out time to read this wonderful prayer book, and if you have an extra second, I would love to hear what you think about this book.

Please, do share your testimonies with me by sending emails to pastor@prayermadueke.com, or through the social media at www.facebook.com/prayer.madueke. I invite you also to www.prayermadueke.com to view other books I have written on various issues of life, especially on marriage, family, sexual problems and money.

I will be delighted to partner with you in organized crusades, ceremonies, marriages and Marriage seminars, special events, church ministration and fellowship for the advancement of God's Kingdom here on earth.

Thank you again, and I wish you success in your life.

God bless you.

In Christ,

Prayer M. Madueke

OTHER BOOKS BY PRAYER M. MADUEKE

- *21/40 Nights Of Decrees And Your Enemies Will Surrender*
- *Confront And Conquer*
- *Tears in Prison*
- *35 Special Dangerous Decrees*
- *The Reality of Spirit Marriage*
- *Queen of Heaven*
- *Leviathan the Beast*
- *100 Days Prayer To Wake Up Your Lazarus*
- *Dangerous Decrees To Destroy Your Destroyers*
- *The spirit of Christmas*
- *More Kingdoms To Conquer*
- *Your Dream Directory*
- *The Sword Of New Testament Deliverance*
- *Alphabetic Battle For Unmerited Favors*
- *Alphabetic Character Deliverance*
- *Holiness*
- *The Witchcraft Of The Woman That Sits Upon Many Waters*
- *The Operations Of The Woman That Sits Upon Many Waters*
- *Powers To Pray Once And Receive Answers*
- *Prayer Riots To Overthrow Divorce*
- *Prayers To Get Married Happily*
- *Prayers To Keep Your Marriage Out of Troubles*
- *Prayers For Conception And Power To Retain*
- *Prayer Retreat – Prayers to Possess Your Year*
- *Prayers for Nation Building*
- *Organized student in a disorganized school*
- *Welcome to Campus*
- *Alone with God (10 series)*

CONTACTS

AFRICA
#1 Babatunde close,
Off Olaitan Street, Surulere
Lagos, Nigeria
+234 803 353 0599
pastor@prayermadueke.com

#Plot 1791, No. 3 Ijero Close,
Flat 2, Area 1,
Garki 1 - FCT, Abuja
+234 807 065 4159

IRELAND
Ps Emmanuel Oko
#84 Thornfield Square
Cloudalkin D22
Ireland
Tel: +353 872 820 909, +353 872 977 422
aghaoko2003@yahoo.com

EUROPE/SCHENGEN
Collins Kwame
#46 Felton Road
Barking
Essex IG11 7XZ GB
Tel: +44 208 507 8083, +44 787 703 2386, +44 780 703 6916
aghaoko2003@yahoo.com

Made in the USA
Columbia, SC
25 August 2021